DOING
RESEARCH

T0276708

POCKET STUDY SKILLS

Series Editor: **Kate Williams**,
Oxford Brookes University, UK
Illustrations by Sallie Godwin

For the time-pushed student, the *Pocket Study Skills* pack a lot of advice into a little book. Each guide focuses on a single crucial aspect of study giving you step-by-step guidance, handy tips and clear advice on how to approach the important areas which will continually be at the core of your studies.

Published

POCKET STUDY SKILLS

Gary Thomas

DOING
RESEARCH
SECOND EDITION

BLOOMSBURY ACADEMIC
LONDON • NEW YORK • OXFORD • NEW DELHI • SYDNEY

BLOOMSBURY ACADEMIC
Bloomsbury Publishing Plc
50 Bedford Square, London, WC1B 3DP, UK
1385 Broadway, New York, NY 10018, USA
29 Earlsfort Terrace, Dublin 2, Ireland

BLOOMSBURY, BLOOMSBURY ACADEMIC and the Diana
logo are trademarks of Bloomsbury Publishing Plc

First published 2017 by RED GLOBE PRESS
Reprinted by Bloomsbury Academic, 2022

A catalogue record for this book is available from the British Library.

A catalogue record for this book is available from the Library of Congress.

ISBN: PB: 978-1-1376-0591-7
ePDF: 978-1-1376-0592-4
ePub: 978-1-3503-1526-6

Printed and bound in Great Britain

To find out more about our authors and books visit www.bloomsbury.com and sign up for our newsletters.

Contents

Acknowledgements

I am enormously grateful to Kate Williams, the editor of the Macmillan Pocket Study Skills series, for her idea for this book and her invaluable advice and guidance in improving drafts. Many thanks also to colleagues and students at the University of Birmingham for their guidance and support. Huge thanks to Sallie Godwin for her excellent illustrations, Helen Caunce for stimulating this second edition, the anonymous reviewers of the first edition for their valuable comments, and the editorial and production teams at Macmillan for their detailed work.

1 What is research?

research: *v.* investigate; study; explore; delve into; examine; inquire; seek; look into. *n.* careful search; systematic investigation aimed at increasing the store of knowledge.

We all do research every day: research is just finding something out. Go to the train enquiries website and look up the time of your train – that's research. There's nothing difficult about research.

But when you do research at university something else is involved. The research has to be about something more significant than train times: it's about finding out something *new*. You should be curious to find out an answer. In exploring your subject you have to base your inquiry not only on the information you collect, but also on what is already known about the subject. And your inquiry has to be thorough and *balanced* – in other words, you can't just find out what you want to find out by ignoring any inconvenient facts that you uncover.

And it all has to be done in an order that lets you build from one part to the next in what I call the 'five steps of *research*'.

1. Being curious & wanting to find out something new

2. Looking to see what is already known about the subject by reading around

3. Collecting evidence

4. Using your evidence to build an argument

5. Writing it up to communicate it to others

All this, from beginning to end – from the first question to reading around to conducting your own inquiries 'out in the field' – is *research*.

And why do you need this book? You need this book because students often, too often, begin by ploughing straight into interviews or questionnaires or whatever, without really being sure why they are doing them or what they are going to end up with. Good research design helps you to join the dots and end up with a meaningful piece of research: a piece of research that will get you an 'A'.

2 Where do I start?

Get a piece of paper and write down:

- *An idea* – about something that interests you, or something that is important to you in your work or your studies. (Don't worry about getting it perfect at this stage. We will refine this later.) This is what you want to research into.
- *A timetable*. You don't need much on it right now, just the date you will start and the date you have to hand in your work. (We'll fill in more details later.)

This will do for now. You have started. Marvellous! You know what you want to research into and you have a time by which you have to have completed your research project.

3 Where do I get an idea from?

Ideas can come from anywhere, such as:

▶ a topic you have found interesting in your lectures
▶ an issue at work or on a placement
▶ an item in the news
▶ something you have discussed with your friends
▶ brainstorming with friends or family.

If none of this works, try:

▶ googling websites of big government departments such as education or health
▶ putting 'Campbell Collaboration library' into Google to find hot topics in social scientific research
▶ going through the alphabet to see what topics come up as you go from A to Z. For example, 'A' might give you 'Acid rain', 'Autism' or 'Assistants in schools'; 'B' might give 'Boot camps', 'Botulism and Botox', 'Brazil's street children' or 'Behaviour management'; 'C' might give 'Criminal justice' and 'Clinical excellence', and so on. Try it with friends on a long journey instead of 'I Spy'. Fun!

4 What next?

The beginning is your idea; the end is when you hand in your completed project.

So, let's fill in the path between beginning and end. Let's unpack this, which involves getting the bits out of the research package. Those bits comprise what is often called the research *design*.

The design

There is nothing magical about design. Designing research is like designing anything else – a bathroom, a kitchen or anything: there will be things you need for whatever it is you are designing – a bath,

taps, a basin. You have to decide how much you want to spend. You need to consider the space available and where the water and drains are located. You need to decide

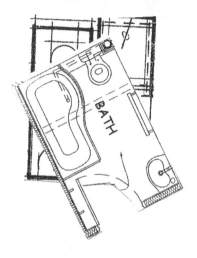

when the work is going to be done, who will help you and what you can do yourself. All this comprises the design of the bathroom.

Designing your research is just the same. You need to think about when to start and when to end and when you have time free to work on the project. You have to decide what tools you need to do the job – tools such as questionnaires, interviews or statistics. You need to think about how you will analyse the information you get from these tools and how you will present it. All this is the design. All these bits will be carefully put together by you to make the final research project.

Questions, questions

When you are told to do a *research project* at university, it is rather different from when you are told to do an *essay* or an *assignment*. With the essay or assignment you are *given* a question you have to answer, or at least a topic area to address.

But it's harder when you have to think of the question yourself. Questions, questions. There are so many of them. Finding one you can reasonably answer is your first challenge.

It's important that the question is about filling a gap in knowledge. But it should also be manageable. If you fancy a steak you don't go and bite a cow. (Apologies to vegetarians. I'm one, by the way.) You buy the right-sized piece, cook it how you like it, cut it up and stick it in your mouth. The same is true of research: you can't solve all the answers of the world, so you have to choose a manageable question and answer it in a way that suits you. Let's have a look at some questions to see what might be good or bad about them as *research questions*.

Your research question ✓ or ✗

Questions	Is this a good research question?
What are the moons of Mars called?	✗ No. You can just look it up in a book. It doesn't involve new knowledge.
Why do children fail to learn to read?	✗ No. This is too wide a question. There are probably as many answers as there are children who can't read.

How far was the Second World War caused by the First World War?	✓ Yes. It's a big question, but it allows you to suggest an answer and find evidence to support it.
Why does Abbi seem to 'switch off' when she has to do maths?	✓ Yes. It's just Abbi you are concerned about – not all children. So you can suggest possible answers and then seek evidence to support those possible answers.
How did the varroa mite affect the honeybee population in the decade 2000–2010?	✓ Yes. It's a limited timespan that you can look at in detail and data will be readily available.

I hope you can see that a research question has to be:

▶ about finding new knowledge
▶ specific – not too broad
▶ answerable with the resources available to you
▶ answerable with reasoning and evidence.

Your **question** will emerge out of your **initial idea**, but the actual question will narrow down the initial idea. It will draw a border around it and enable you to focus on it. If you find it hard moving from idea to question, remember Rudyard Kipling's poem from *The elephant's child*:

> I keep six honest serving-men
> (They taught me all I knew);
> Their names are What and Why and When
> And How and Where and Who.

In other words, think of these questions framing your initial interest. Remember that 'what', 'when', 'where' and 'who' lead to descriptive answers, while 'why' and 'how' often lead to answers that are about explanation. Explanation is clearly trickier than description, and we'll come on to this in a moment. (See also *Getting critical* in this series for ways of using these key questions.)

First you need a *first question* ... and then you need a *final question*

First questions develop into final questions. You hone them until they're just right. Actually, a better phrase than 'first question' is *prima facie question*. Now I can see my readers' eyes glazing over: Latin. 'Why prima facie?' I can hear you saying.

Sorry. It's nothing technical. It's just such a useful way of describing what you need to do when you start out with your question. 'Prima facie' just means 'at first look'. It's useful because in most research, and certainly in research in the social sciences, your 'first look' question changes in the course of your work. You start with your first, naive question, right at the beginning. You then read about the topic and maybe do some initial observations and inquiries, and after all this your question changes. So, you have:

▶ your first question, which I call your **prima facie question**, and
▶ your final question, which I call … er … your **final question**.

So, the sequence is:

⟨ ▶ Have an idea … have a prima facie question.
↖ ▶ Do some groundwork: read around, ask questions, do preliminary inquiries, think about the question some more, then
⟨ ▶ Write out your final question – this comes after you have done your groundwork,
↖ which I discuss in Part 2.

Now that you have your questions sorted out, you can be a bit more precise about your schedule for doing the research. Remember that research isn't one process; it's a collection of processes knitted together and you need to do the processes in the right order.

Let's say that you have to do a 10,000-word project that counts for a double module in your university. You have from 1 January to 1 June to complete it. The first thing to say is: don't leave it all until 15 May. This would be a bad idea. Break it up and draw a timeline like this one.

	Jan	Feb	Mar	Apr	May	June
Come up with a question	▬					
Review literature and do desk research	▬▬▬▬▬ ▪▪▪▪▪▪▪▪▪▪▪					
Revise question and explore method		▬▬▬ ▪▪▪▪▪				
Do fieldwork			▬▬▬▬▬▬▬			
Analyse findings				▬▬▬▬▬▬		
Write up and hand in					▬▬▬▬	

Notice that some of the processes overlap. Notice also that you go in and out of some processes (dotted lines), as the need arises.

6 Checklist for planning

1 Have you had an idea?	What is it? Describe it here.
2 Have you got a prima facie question?	What is it? Jot it down here.
3 Have you drawn a timeline?	Yes or No

To get from your prima facie question to a final question you have to do some work. It's like the bulldozers clearing a building site before a new house is built. They have to clear the ground. And so do you: you have to clear the ground. You need some kit for this: a **literature review** and a **storyboard**, and you also need to consider **ethics**.

The ground clearing means rethinking your initial question and doing a bit of toing and froing. It involves what is sometimes called a 'recursive design' to your research. The alternative is a linear design, which is more usual in certain of the sciences such as physics or chemistry. However, in the social sciences and the applied sciences it is usual for the research, as it is being done, to influence the shape of the ultimate research. As you research you find stuff out and it affects the way you proceed.

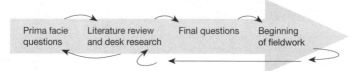

This diagram isn't supposed to look pretty. It's supposed to look a mess. In fact, draw in your own arrows and mess it up even more. The idea I'm trying to convey is that your research changes as you proceed: you'll have new ideas and these will influence the direction and progress of your research – these are the backward arrows on the diagram. They're not 'bad' backward arrows; they're backward in the sense of letting you think again – letting you refine your initial questions.

Once you are beyond the right-hand side of the diagram, though, do try to keep on the ⟶ straight and narrow. Recursiveness has its limits. In other words, do go into your research with an open mind, knowing that you will be changing and varying, but once you have decided, be decisive and go for it.

Let's have a look in more detail at those metaphorical bulldozers, the literature review and the storyboard.

7 A literature review

The main reason for the **literature review** is to find out what has already been done. This provides a raft on which you can build your research. Without the raft, it would be much more difficult to float your research.

The literature review enables you to say 'Evans and Adams have found this', 'There's a gap here', 'Bloggs is disagreeing with Smith; I wonder why that is', 'Brown and Patel both say this, but it disagrees with the general scientific view', or 'public opinion is disputed by Davies, who says …' or something else like this.

The literature review fills in the gaps in your knowledge, or, indeed, it may create some new gaps for you. It is sometimes called 'desk research', because it may also include other kinds of preliminary investigation that you can do sitting at your desk. You may, for example, wish to look at some statistics about your subject: if you were interested in the increase in the incidence of the 'superbug' MRSA, you might look at the official statistics over the last 10 years to see if you could discern any kind of 'shape' in the increase – it might have accelerated, or, by contrast, slowed down in recent years.

Now, as you do your literature review, or desk research, you will almost certainly think about changing your prima facie question. This is normal; don't worry about it. In fact, it is more than normal: it is necessary. It's part of the *clearing the ground* process. It is necessary that you should revisit your question – that you should say:

> 'Oh, I hadn't thought of that.'
> 'Oh, that has already been done by Bloggs, so I won't bother.'
> 'Oh, no one has looked at this; I think I'll look at this instead.'

In other words, the literature review helps you to refine your question. The website www.engageinresearch.ac.uk/index.html (very good for scientists) gives the example that you may have had a prima facie question about the control of the pine weevil in a forestry situation. It makes the case that the literature review could help you to focus this in such a way that you restrict your final question to one that was on method of pesticide application.

When you are reading, you have to find out information quickly. Do this in the following ways.

- Use Google, Google Scholar and Google Books. With Google Scholar and Google Books you can actually find bits of the book or article that are probably the most relevant for what you want to find out.
- Speed read – don't think you have to read every word. Many academic books are not well written and it would drive you barmy to try to read and understand every word. 'Gut' articles and books by reading the abstract (in an article) or the back cover (of a book), then skim through quickly. Look for material that is relevant to your question.
- Always keep your question in mind as you do your reading, and ask: 'How does this article/book/source relate to my research question?'
- Copy and paste key bits into a Word file, recording where you found the work, the author, title and other details and the key points. Put different references in new paragraphs (see *Referencing and understanding plagiarism* in this series).
- When you are in a webpage, use the *Find* facility (Ctrl F) to find key words in the material you are reading.
- Always be critical of what you are reading. The person who wrote it is only human, like you or me. If it doesn't make sense, shout at it. It's the author's fault if you haven't understood, not yours, so they deserve to be shouted at (but do remember the neighbours). Try reading it once more, but if it doesn't make sense the second time, move on quickly.

- Use 'sticky notes' to highlight key pages of books and printed articles. Put the note at the place where the key text occurs on the page.
- If you don't already know, ask the librarian to show you how to use the most up-to-date way of accessing articles from your computer, tablet or smartphone. All university libraries will give you access, free, to just about any journal in the world. (Don't ever be tempted to pay good money for an article you find on a publisher's website via Google.) Actually, your university is paying for access to the journals, and you are paying a lot to the university. So, I'll rephrase the bit about it being free: *since you are paying for it, make sure you use it*.

Useful resources in literature searching

I have already mentioned Google Scholar and Google Books, but there are other more specialised websites that you can use to search the literature.

The Web of Science (formerly Web of Knowledge)

This major resource gives access to the top-rated journals, divided according to academic disciplines. You can log in to the Web of Science only if your university subscribes (although nearly all do). Type 'Web of Science' into the library search box and look for the answer that comes up with 'Thomson Scientific'. Once you are at the Web of Science home page and you are asked which databases you want to search (under the dropdown box labelled 'All Databases'), click the option labelled 'Web of Science™ Core Collection'. You'll be able to search by topic and/or by author. There is an official Thomson Scientific tutorial on how to use it. To find this, type 'Web of Science quick tour' into your search engine.

Zetoc

Zetoc gives access to the British Library's 20,000 journals and 16,000 conference proceedings published every year. It will give you alerts to relevant material.

The Library of Congress catalogue

Useful for checking bibliographic details of hard-to-find books.

EThOS

EThOS is the British Library's digital repository of all doctoral theses completed at UK institutions. Use it to find theses on your topic.

Specific subject sources

There are many subject-specific databases. These include ERIC for education, PubMed for biomedical literature, CINAHL for nursing and PsycINFO for psychologists. To review these to see which would be useful for you, go to your library webpages.

Reference managers

ERIC, PubMed and Web of Science will enable you to export citations directly into reference management programs such as *EndNote*, *Reference Manager* or *ProCite*. Your university library will have webpages that explain how to use these. Reference managers such as these will organise all your references for you and even format them for you. (See *Referencing and understanding plagiarism* in this series, Chapter 3 and Part 3.)

Once you have your information from your literature searches, you need to make sense of it and knit it into a meaningful story. One of the big problems of students' literature reviews is that they look like lists (Bloggs says X; Jones says Y; Smith says Z) rather than stories. (See also *Where's your argument?* and *Planning your dissertation* in this series.)

Your literature review should be more like a story than a list. You should be connecting this bit with that bit, saying how this fits but that doesn't, and showing how there is a theme (or not) through the literature you are reviewing. If, inconveniently, there is *not* a theme, say so and then suggest some reasons why this might be.

Don't be fazed by the differences in opinion that you find. Take pleasure in them, and use them to understand your field of study. As in any human endeavour, there are disagreements, rivalries, conflicts, friendships and even cabals among professional researchers. Try to understand why these exist: try to create a story and explain the story. Then, use your understanding to modify your initial questions. You can then progress from here.

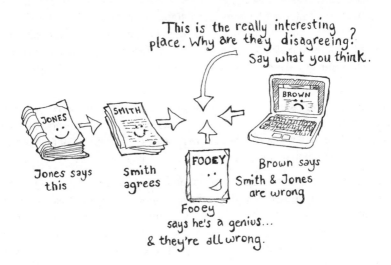

Jones says this

Smith agrees

This is the really interesting place. Why are they disagreeing? Say what you think.

BROWN

Brown says Smith & Jones are wrong

FOOEY

Fooey says he's a genius... & they're all wrong.

8 Drawing storyboards

A **storyboard** helps you to get a mental map of the subject you intend to study. Just to illustrate the point: suppose that you are studying Goldilocks's psychology. What was her motivation in making a visit to the three bears' house? This isn't a very clearly defined issue or question as it stands. A storyboard will enable you to think about some of the issues surrounding Goldilocks's walk.

This example shows you how easy it is to come up with fruitful avenues of inquiry on almost anything. You have a range of directions almost immediately. You could focus on the food side, looking at whether she was hungry because she was greedy or whether she was underfed. You could focus on the child welfare issues: what were her parents doing? It's surely disgraceful that a small girl should be left on her own in a forest, especially one known to be populated by bears – wait till the *Daily Mail* finds out. Or maybe she deliberately got lost: maybe she had something of a wanderlust and she had gone against her parents' strict instructions. Maybe she wasn't the paragon of virtue portrayed in all the storybooks; maybe she was a little tearaway. We just don't know. This opens a rich vein of inquiry about Goldilocks's psychology, challenging received wisdom.

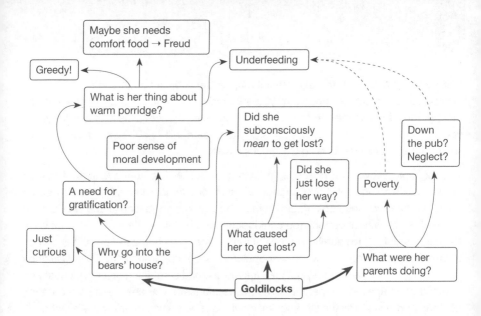

I hope you can see that even using this example we can draw into the storyboard some quite interesting potential avenues of exploration, each of them offering separate lines of questioning and separate sources of evidence towards a solution. Sadly, we know so little about the real Goldilocks: there isn't a huge amount of literature about Goldilocks's parents' income or her taste in food. But in a real example, that knowledge will exist in the literature.

So, potential lines of reasoning open up to you as you do the work. As you have been doing your literature review and drawing your storyboards, you will have been thinking very hard about your research topic. You'll be able to say: 'I want to do X', or 'No, I don't want to do X any more, I want to find out about Y.'

What you must now do is to establish and make clear how your argument will proceed.

The first thing to do in setting out your likely argument is to establish the problem in the ground you have cleared. You have straightened things out a bit. Now you can be clear about where the issues lie.

Finding an angle

This is often the weakest point in student research (and, indeed, much research conducted by professional researchers and academics). I call it the 'so what?' problem. You are looking at the use of information technology in the classroom. *So what?* You are looking at how dentists use their hygienists. *So what?* You are looking at the control of vine weevils by pesticides. *So what?*

The topic has to be interesting and meaningful to the reader: it has to relate to something that conspicuously will benefit from research, so that no one can say 'So what?' Your question therefore has to be set in a context that establishes an issue or an **angle** on a theme. You should be in a position to do this now, because you have – with your literature review and your storyboard – got a good feel for where the issues in the field lie. An excellent book for further reading on this is *The craft of research* by Booth et al. (2008).

Once you know where the issue is, you can promise a way of looking at it. You can now explain the ultimate direction you have decided to take in your research:

1 First, you need to explain that you have established some common ground on which everyone agrees.
2 Then you have to point out that there is a problem or an issue. (Perhaps people disagree on how to deal with something that emerges from the common ground.)
3 Then you need to propose an angle from which you will address this problem or issue.
4 Then you need to promise some kind of answer.

The opening context will contain some common ground on which everyone can agree. The problem or 'angle' contains two parts:

1 some missing evidence or contradictory reasoning, and
2 the consequences of not having an answer.

The response concerns your promise of a solution.

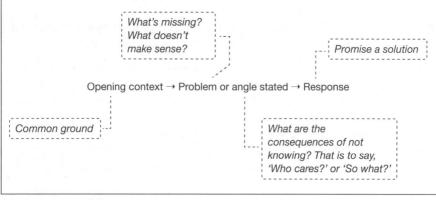

Let's have a look at this in a real-life issue: the inclusion of children with learning difficulties into ordinary schools.

General stages	Specific proposals
1 You need to establish some **common ground** on which everyone agrees.	Everyone agrees that inclusion, equity and diversity are good things.
2 You have to point out that there is a **problem** or an **issue**. (Perhaps people disagree on how to deal with something that emerges from the common ground.)	Some people say that these values should guide the way we structure the school system: all children should be educated together. Others say that this is impossible. They say that children with serious difficulties cannot practically be taught next to those with no problems. In particular, children will tend to bully those with special needs.
3 You need to propose an **angle** from which you will address this problem or issue. The angle may offer a frame for explaining the problem.	What is the actual experience of a child who has difficulties in one of today's classrooms?
4 You need to **promise some kind of answer**.	I am going to look in detail at the inclusion of a child with Down syndrome in an ordinary primary school class over a period of one week. It will be a snapshot case study where I observe the behaviour of the class towards her and her reactions to this. It will contribute to the debate about the practical possibility of inclusion.

You will be outlining points 1–4 above in your Introduction chapter. Then, right at the end of your literature review, you need a section that summarises the review and revisits these questions in the light of the review, also stating your final question.

In any research involving people, you must think about questions such as:

- Is there any discomfort for the participants?
- Are you invading participants' privacy?
- Do you have the right to take up people's time?
- Might you be damaging the standing or reputation of participants or others?

Matters such as these are called *risks*, and an assessment of them will form the basis of your university's judgement of the ethical risks of your research proposal in the process of *ethics clearance*.

Getting ethics clearance

This clearance goes under different names in different places, but will usually be called *ethics clearance* or *institutional review*. You will have to write an outline of your proposed research, which will be looked at by a group known as the 'ethics committee' or, more commonly in the USA, the 'institutional review board'.

In the process of ethical clearance, you will need to think about the risks in your research (if there are any) and also the extent to which any risk can be minimised. You will need to weigh any risks against the benefits of your research. You should be prepared to outline these and make a good case for your research.

Universities have their own codes of conduct for research, and webpages outlining procedures for gaining ethics clearance. Professional organisations also have policies and guidelines on ethical research. You can find the ethical codes for relevant organisations online.

In getting ethical clearance, you may be asked about the specific risks and benefits of the research, confidentiality and anonymity, data security and informed consent.

The risks

When you are asked about risks, you should be prepared to talk about:

- the possible psychological, physical, social, legal or economic harm that could come from the research, and any arrangements you have put in place to manage that risk
- any immediate benefits to participants
- possible risks to you as a researcher, and what you are doing to minimise these.

While most situations will not, of course, present any danger, some may. If you are meeting people who are strangers, for example, always take a mobile phone with you and let a friend or family member know where you are going, whom you are meeting, and when you will be expected back.

Confidentiality and anonymity

You should always treat any information provided to you as confidential, taking care at all times not to breach or compromise that confidentiality. Anonymity can be ensured by changing participants' names as well as the name of any institutions (such as schools) to which they are affiliated and the regions in which they are situated. You can give pseudonyms or code numbers to achieve this.

Data security and stewardship

You have a responsibility to keep the data you collect about people secure. Here are some principles of good stewardship of data:

▶ Only use data for the purposes for which they were collected – not for other purposes.
▶ Keep data for a set length of time. For most undergraduate research it will be appropriate to destroy raw data immediately after your project is completed and marked; however, for some research (e.g. that which is part of a clinical

programme, which a postgraduate project may be part of), professional codes of conduct may specify that data must be kept for several years.

▶ Keep the data anonymous.
▶ Use passwords for any files that contain names or personal data, even if they are anonymised.
▶ Don't pass the data on to anyone else.

Informed consent

Informed consent is about the agreement of people to take part in the study *and* their understanding of what they are agreeing to. Informed consent includes the following:

1 Information about the study, including:
   – the nature and purpose of the study, including its methods
   – expected benefits of the study
   – harm (if any) that may follow from the study
   – procedures for ensuring confidentiality, including processes for ensuring anonymity
   – how data will be kept secure
   – how long data will be kept
   – ethics codes being adhered to (e.g. those of the university or a professional body)
   – confirmation that involvement in the project is voluntary and that participants are free to withdraw at any time

- arrangements for debriefing and feedback
- your full name and full contact details.

2 The presentation of (1) in an understandable way, explaining any unusual terms in non-technical language.

3 The option for a potential participant to choose to take part or not.

All this can be provided on an **information sheet** for participants. Where involvement is less complicated, a simple *letter* may be all that is needed, as long as it covers these issues simply. If the project involves any degree of discomfort for participants, they should also be asked to sign a **consent form**.

Opting-in versus implied consent	
Opting-in consent	**Implied consent**
Participants have to make an active choice about becoming involved in the research. You would have to offer an invitation to participants to become involved, preferably in writing, requesting that they return a form indicating willingness to participate. Alternatively, some other *active* choice of the participant would have to be involved, as would be the case in returning a questionnaire.	Sometimes called 'opting-out consent', this is when you tell participants about the research and assume that they give their consent unless they tell you otherwise.

1 Have you done a literature review?	What are the main themes, agreements and disagreements? Write them down here.
2 Have you drawn a storyboard?	What are the 'stories' that emerge? Which will you follow? Jot them down here.
3 Have you looked for an angle?	In two or three paragraphs, summarise what the existing research is *and then say how your research will contribute to resolving an issue in it.*

4 Have you reviewed your prima facie questions in the light of the literature review?	Write down your final question, relating it to the 'angle' in 3.
5 Have you considered ethics (if you are working with people)?	Find the ethics clearance procedures for your university, which will be available on your department or school website. Think about ethics risks, how to minimise them, and issues such as informed consent, confidentiality and data security.

BUILDING A SCAFFOLD

You have to build a scaffold, or frame, to support your research. The scaffold can be one of a variety of shapes and sizes and it will be built to guide the way your research develops.

Another term for these scaffolds that shape your research is **design frames**. Let's have a look at the ones most frequently used in small-scale and undergraduate research:

- action research
- case study
- ethnography
- experiment
- survey.

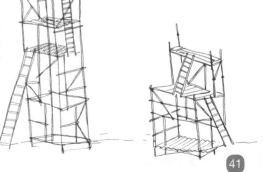

These are all governed by different assumptions about the world and so you have to follow particular ground rules when you adopt them. I won't go into a lot of detail about these now, since there are bigger books that can explain them more fully (e.g. Thomas 2017).

However, I'll begin by saying a little about approaches to research, about ways of judging its trustworthiness, and about sampling. I think you will find it helpful to know something about these general issues so that you can understand the different starting (and ending) points to different design frames.

Let me first distinguish between two broad approaches to research – different approaches to 'finding out':

1 **Quantitative** (also called 'positivist') **research** is where the researcher explores relationships between and among variables using numeric data.

2 **Qualitative** (also called 'interpretivist') **research** is conducted in naturalistic settings that generate data largely from observations and interviews.

The **quantitative approach**, adopted usually in the natural sciences and, to a lesser extent, in the social sciences, assumes that research is best done by standing back from our subjects of study and trying to be impartial, detached and disinterested. Here, we try to reduce the subjects of our study to variables, measuring *quantitatively* – that is, in numbers – how things change in one circumstance or another.

The **qualitative approach**, used more in the social sciences and the humanities, where the study is usually of people, says we have to become part of the situations we are studying. Far from trying to be objective, we should ourselves become *participants* on the research stage, using our insights *as people* in order to understand the behaviour and motivations of the people who are part of those situations. We should value our subjectivity rather than denying it. Here, our data comprise our reflections on the behaviour or the words of those people – they are *qualitative*.

I've noted these two approaches to research since you might think it is strange to find professional researchers using these very different – seemingly contradictory – ideas about finding out. In particular, with the qualitative approach you may feel that it is illegitimate to be *subjective* in anything as systematic as research. Believe me, it's not illegitimate: it's now considered quite appropriate to use one approach for one kind of question, and another approach for a different sort of question. It depends what you want to find out: it's horses for courses.

I'm telling you about this before I start discussing different design frames because you need to understand the variety and diversity of research methods and the legitimacy of these different forms of finding out. I'm also telling you about them because research has its value and its trustworthiness assessed on two important criteria, called **reliability** and **validity**.

With these criteria, we are saying: 'Is this research up to the job? Is it fit for purpose?' These questions are going to be answered differently depending on the approach to 'finding out' that you have adopted. Let me say a little about reliability and validity and how the nature of these criteria change under the different approaches.

Assessing the value and trustworthiness of research

Reliability

Reliability is about the consistency and dependability of a data-gathering procedure. In other words, it's about the extent to which a research instrument such as a test will give the same result in different situations. You have to ask yourself if the data-gathering instruments you have used will give consistent findings across a range of situations.

Validity

Validity is about the degree to which the data you collect and the findings you emerge with provide accurate, meaningful answers to your research questions:

▶ Are the data-gathering instruments you intend to use really the best ones for collecting information on the focus of your study?
▶ Are they going to deliver *valid* findings?

- Are the methods of analysis you are using the best possible ones in the circumstances?
- Will they offer meaningful treatment of the data?
- Will you be able to generalise from your sample to a wider population?

Think about these questions when you are considering data collection and analysis methods.

Validity in qualitative research

Many researchers doing qualitative research question the whole notion of validity (and, to a lesser extent, reliability). How can it be appropriate, they ask, to foreground issues such as the adequacy of a sample when they are not attempting to generalise from a sample to a wider population?

Instead, they look at the quality of the evidence being provided and the way this evidence is used to support the claims of the researcher. We should judge the claims of qualitative research, they say, in terms of:

- **plausibility** – judging the analysis and the claims according to how they fit in with the findings of other research and what we already know, and
- **credibility** – judging how far the claims are based on forms of data gathering and analysis that are not likely to be prone to significant distortion or error.

A note on sampling and selection

In social research, we often want to find out something that we can say is relevant to a whole group of people – called a **population**. However, we're not often able to study the *whole* population since we would need huge resources of time and energy to study this many people. So, instead, we study a **sample** – a group selected from the whole population – and we try to draw inferences about the whole population from this sample.

As you'll realise, the sample has to do a lot of heavy lifting here. If it is to help us in our aim, much will depend on the quality of this sample. How far is a sample capable of representing the whole population? If, for example, you were interested in students' study habits and you took as your sample the first 10 students you met in the bar on Tuesday lunchtime and gave them a questionnaire, you would be unlikely to get any valid findings. Why? Because habitual bar-dwellers are unlikely to be representative of the student population at large (let alone its study habits), so the findings you made would not be generalisable to the population. You need to take steps to make the sample as representative as possible.

But the representativeness of the sample is more important in some kinds of research than in others. Clearly, it is important if we want to generalise to a whole population. However, generalisation is not always the point. In action research and case study, for example (which we'll look at in Chapters 13 and 14), the point is to inform particular circumstances and gain insights from the in-depth study that we undertake in these detailed studies. The *selection* of the subject to study is more the issue: Is the subject we select likely to tell us something useful? Sample representativeness is usually of little or no significance in such research.

Or, in other circumstances, generalisation may be important, but the practical demands of the research scenario mean that access – simply finding enough people – is an even more important consideration. These issues are summarised in the table below.

Types of sample or selection and when they are used

Purpose	Type of sample or selection	Features
Where representativeness is central	Random sample	Large number of individuals selected randomly from the population
	Stratified sample	Grouping a population into subgroups (or 'strata') by certain characteristics (e.g. level of highest qualification), and drawing from these strata in proportion to their size in the whole population

Where representativeness is a factor, but access is even more pressing	Convenience sample	Using the most easily accessible people to participate in a study
	Snowball sample	Study participants themselves refer the researcher to other individuals who fit the study criteria
	Purposive sample	The researcher selects participants who are considered on an a priori basis to be typical of the wider population
Where representativeness is less important and the selection of a key subject is more important	Case selection	A subject is chosen on the basis of its likely capacity for revealing interesting information

In a small student project it's unlikely that you will have the resources to construct a large, random sample or a stratified sample. It's much more likely that you will need to go for one of the easier but less robust (in representativeness terms) types of sample, such as the convenience, the snowball or the purposive. And remember, if you are doing a case study (bottom row in the table above), the selection of the individual case is made on grounds of potential fruitfulness of meaning rather than representativeness.

13 Action research

The clue's in the name. You guessed: it's about action. And research. The idea is that you are *doing* something (there's the action) and you want to do whatever it is better. So you *research* (there's the research) into it – into your practice.

Clearly, this is easier if you have a practice – usually in a job – to improve. For students without a relevant job it may not seem to be the most appropriate design frame. Do think about it, though, because if you are doing a part-time job, for example as a care worker in a home for old people, it may well be that there is an aspect of your work that you could use as the basis of a research project at university. Maybe Mrs Jones and two or three other residents are not joining in with the social activity that is organised for them. The action research project would begin with a prima facie question such as: 'How can I change my practice in such a way that Mrs Jones's life is improved?'

The short way to describe action research is that it is like a coil: you move onwards and upwards along the coil, learning from each thing you do before proceeding on to the next step.

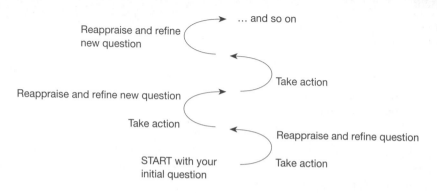

Reappraise and refine
new question

... and so on

Take action

Reappraise and refine new question

Take action

Reappraise and refine question

START with your
initial question

Take action

You'll see that the pattern is: action → reappraise → action and so on. The action you take will be something that you think may improve your practice. In the Mrs Jones example this might be taking two minutes to talk to Mrs Jones each day. The 'reappraise' element would include gathering some data (see p. 47) to assess any effect, prior to taking another action, or amending or extending the current one.

Good further reading on action research is McNiff (2016).

14   Case study

Case study is a study of one thing in its entirety. You are not trying to break up the world into variables that you aim to measure independently. Rather, you are looking in detail at the whole situation.

In the table below, you can see how case study compares with another widely used design frame, the survey. You will notice that in case study the idea is to look at a large number of interrelating features of each case, whereas with the survey you look at a small number of features of each case.

The 'case' of case study is like a container – think of your suit**case** – and the interesting thing about this is the way that your suit**case** *contains* a whole range of things. In your own suitcase this will be your flip-flops, toothbrush, camera, jeans, etc. In a piece of research it will be the context, the people and the time.

So, if you were interested in the experience of patients waiting in a doctor's waiting room, the study would be defined by an aspect of this. It might be of one room itself, or it might be a study of one person attending a waiting room. It's up to you to decide what defines 'the case' of the case study. Is it *this waiting room* as a particularly

DOING RESEARCH

	Case study	Survey
Investigates ...	one case or a small number of cases	a large number of cases
Data collected and analysed about ...	a large number of features of each case	a small number of features of each case
Study of ...	naturally occurring cases where the aim is *not* to control variables	naturally occurring cases selected to maximise the sample's representativeness of a wider population
Quantification of data ...	is not a priority	is a priority

Source: Adapted from Hammersley and Gomm (2000)

interesting waiting room (because it is especially good or bad), or is it *one person's* experience in a waiting room?

If you focused on the room itself, you would want to look at features such as the dimensions, the 'feel' (clinical or warm), the entrance, the pictures on the wall and so on, but you would also be wanting to assess people's experiences in the room, by, for example, interviewing them. If, by contrast, you were looking at one person's experience, you might ask them to jot down all the anxieties, doubts and reassurances they felt as they entered and exited the room.

You can probably see from this example that there are two parts to a case study: the **subject** (that is, the case itself – the particular waiting room here), and the **object**, which is the analytical frame that the case will be illuminating – in the example here, the experience of patients in the room. How, in other words, can the subject illustrate or help you to explain patients' experiences? You will have chosen this particular waiting room because it is a good example of what you hope to reveal in your study. The subject, in a sense, serves the object of the study.

The case study cannot be simply a description of something: to be research (rather than just illustration), it must have an analytical purpose – an object.

Good further reading on case study are *How to do your case study* (Thomas 2016) and *Analyzing a case study* in this series.

15 Ethnography

'Ethnography' is from the Greek *ethnos*, meaning folk, so ethnography means 'study of folk'. The word came to be used for a new type of social inquiry early in the twentieth century – one that said that if we are studying people (as distinct from nitrogen or pulleys), we should use our own ready-made strengths as researchers, namely, that we are *people*. Yes, you are a person; I am a person.

We shouldn't try to bury this fact and aim to be objective and invisible as social researchers. We should become part of the situation we are studying. The term **participant observation** is therefore sometimes used to describe the way ethnography works. What is the toolkit of the participant observer? It involves:

▶ *keeping a diary*: doing ethnography involves regularly keeping notes on all that is happening
▶ *talking naturally with others*: finding out from others what they think just by normal talking
▶ *observing naturally*: looking to see what people are doing, and taking notes.

After you have done any or all of this, your job as an ethnographic researcher is to make sense of it (see Part 5). Good examples of ethnography in social inquiry can be found in *An anthropologist on Mars* (Sacks 1996), and in the article, 'Deep play: notes on the Balinese cockfight', by the great anthropologist Clifford Geertz (in Geertz 1975).

An experiment in everyday terms can mean simply an informal trial. I might say: 'I'm going to do a little experiment to see if the geranium likes it better on the other windowsill.' This is fine and may give me a result worth having: the geranium might indeed do better on the other windowsill.

But this isn't a very well designed experiment. To qualify scientifically, the experiment has to be a bit better thought through. It means looking at all the possible factors, or *variables*, that might affect the growth of the geranium, and then changing one – and only one – of them while holding everything else constant to assess the effect of your *one* change. The vocabulary used to describe this is as follows:

▶ the thing being changed is the **independent variable**
▶ the thing we are interested in as an 'outcome', in this case, the health of the geranium, is the **dependent variable**.

We have to have *measures* of the effects of the changes, such as growth in millimetres, or changes in leaf colour.

Let's look at my little experiment again in these terms.

to see if the geranium likes it better on the other windowsill

This is the dependent variable: whether the geranium 'likes it better'. We decide to measure this by (say) its growth in millimetres.

This is the independent variable: *place* – the windowsills. We would need to keep a systematic record of the places we had moved it to.

So, a scientific experiment involves this systematic changing of one variable while you control the others. Your change might be in giving a drug versus not giving it, or it might be in giving extra tuition versus not giving it. The comparison of the 'giving' versus the 'not giving' is usually done in professional research by using two different groups – one getting the treatment and one not. Or it might be done by subjecting one group to two different conditions.

This would be difficult (but not impossible) to do properly with the poorly geranium. We would need a goodly number – say 20 – of sickly geraniums, all of which had been on the one windowsill. We would then divide the group into two and put half on the new windowsill (perhaps facing west), while the others, which we call the *control group*, we leave on the first windowsill (which perhaps faced north). The table shows this more clearly.

	Pre-test	Treatment	Post-test	
Experiment group (of sickly geraniums)	✐ Take first measure of height	✓ **move** to new windowsill	✐ Take second measure of height a week later	(You hope)
Control group (of sickly geraniums)	✐ Take first measure of height	✗ **don't move** to new windowsill	✐ Take second measure of height a week later	(Oh dear)

Note that this experiment has had a positive outcome. We can't always (or even usually) expect this.

An alternative 'real-world' experiment design would be repeatedly to move the one geranium – one week on the first windowsill, then one week on the new windowsill, then back again and so on. (This would approximate to something called a 'repeated measures' design, or 'crossover' design.) This way, the geranium is acting as its *own* control. But there would be all sorts of problems with this design, such as maturation of the plant, natural light levels changing over time – in other words, everything else would *not* be constant. This is one of the annoying things about experimenting with living things – geraniums or people, as distinct from pulleys and nitrogen – and why social scientists in particular have to be so careful with experimental design.

It is quite difficult to set up an experiment in undergraduate research, but not impossible. Indeed, if you are a psychology undergraduate, setting up some kind of experiment is almost certain to be part of your practical course. You will be comparing groups of people or groups of animals rather than geraniums, and because of constraints of time and money they will be fairly small groups. The significance of any differences you find will need to be assessed using a statistical test. Here you would need to look for two *non-parametric tests*: the Mann–Whitney test and the Wilcoxon rank-sum test. You'll find out how to use them in *Discovering statistics using IBM SPSS statistics* (Field 2013).

In Chapter 12, I talked about ways in which we can judge the validity of different kinds of research. It's worth saying here that experimental research is such a specialised yet broad field that there are special concerns about validity.

There are many features of an experiment that, if they are not thought through thoroughly, can affect the soundness of the findings. The most obvious of these are:

▶ the extent to which the groups being compared are equivalent, and
▶ the extent to which you have been able to control all the variables that may be at play in the experimental situation.

If an experiment attends to these features and, as far as possible, deals with them, it is said to have good **internal validity**.

There is also **external validity**. This is the degree to which the results of a study can be generalised beyond your sample to an entire population – to other people, places or times. You have to ask yourself how truly representative your sample is of this wider population for such generalisations to be possible.

17 Survey

You have heard of surveys, I'm sure. The trouble is, many people think that *survey* means the same as *research*, but it doesn't. A survey is a *type* of research frame, that is, one of our scaffolds, in which you collect information from a number of people – the more the better. You ask them questions, perhaps in a questionnaire (face to face, over the phone or online), or in an interview, or they may be completing some kind of diary entry (see p. 71).

... er, 'tarantula' isn't on my list

The data can be of all kinds. You collect the information to describe some feature of the situation in which they exist, perhaps the pets they keep, for example, or perhaps to find out about their attitudes. It is all completely static; in other words, these features of the situation are *not changed* in any way, as they would be in an experiment. Once you have collected these data, you can look at them for anything that might be interesting and present the results statistically (see pp. 93–97).

1 Have you thought about your research question?	What question is your research answering? What kind of research will answer it?
2 Have you decided what sort of approach you will take to your research?	Will you principally be using an approach that demands the collection of numbers or words, or both?
3 Have you considered reliability and validity?	Show that you have considered other approaches, but have decided on this one because it seems most reliable and valid.

4 Have you thought about sampling or selection?	Show that you have considered other forms of sampling (or selection) and that you recognise the benefits and drawbacks of the one you are choosing.
5 Have you decided what your design frame is?	What is it? Write it down here.

FIELDWORK: FINDING THE DATA

Doing research at university may mean just finding something out by looking for it in a book. However, when you are asked to do *research* by your tutors, you are usually being expected to find something out **empirically**. This means that you are expected to find something *original* and from *your own experience* (i.e. not a book author's experience). To do this you need to look at the world, ask people questions and keep notes. It means using your eyes and ears.

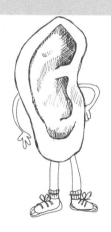
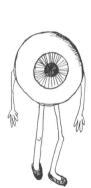

> *Data is plural of 'datum' so we say 'these data'.*

With your eyes and ears you gather **data** (or information) and with these data you can answer your questions and support (or not) the claims you made at the beginning of your research. When data are used in support of a proposition in this way, they become **evidence**. Evidence is very important in research.

The process of collecting data is sometimes called **fieldwork**. Let's look at some of the principal ways you can collect data in your fieldwork. You can collect them through:

- interviews
- diaries
- questionnaires
- observation
- official statistics – also called 'secondary data'.

Let's look at these and how you might use them.

A research interview is a discussion with someone else with a purpose (your purpose, not theirs) in mind. It can be more structured and formal, or less structured and completely informal. The degree of formality is reflected in the three broad types of interview you can do:

1 **A structured interview**. Here, you have your questions written out and you go through them in order and without deviation.
2 **An unstructured interview**. This, by contrast, is completely open. Other than directing your interviewees to the topic you want to talk about, you inject very little else. Your aim is to find out what interviewees think without influencing them too much.
3 **A semi-structured interview**. This is the happy medium. You have an **interview schedule** of themes or topics that you write out on a list in front of you, but beyond this there is no structure. You just make sure that you cover each of the themes on your schedule. The example here is of a simple interview schedule of attitudes to the royal family (RF).

Interview schedule

Subject	Done?
What do you think of the royal family?	✓
Does the RF contribute to our economy?	✓
Does it accentuate or diminish class consciousness?	✓

The semi-structured interview, the 'happy medium', is the form of interview most commonly used by researchers. It's not a straitjacket, so you can deviate from it as necessary, but you make sure you get through the issues you wanted to ask about. You should feel free to modify the questions, or ask supplementary questions. The essence of a semi-structured interview is that the structure reminds you of your aims and themes, but it does not constrain you slavishly to follow a format.

Although it is usually preferred, the semi-structured interview isn't always best. If, for example, you are doing an ethnography (see p. 55), it would be better to use an unstructured interview because your aim in an ethnography is to learn from your research participants unobtrusively.

You can record the interview:
▶ electronically and then copy it all out afterwards (the copy is called a 'transcript')
▶ by taking notes during the interview
▶ by taking notes and recording electronically at the same time.

I find that recording everything and then copying it all out is time-consuming, a bit of a bore and hardly ever worth it. It's much better, in my opinion, to take notes of the important bits and back this up with an electronic copy if necessary. So, take your recorder in with you and record the interview, but don't rely on it: just use it as a back-up to fill in bits you have missed or where you want to remind yourself of something.

Group interviews and focus groups

People behave differently in groups from when they are on their own, and if you decide to interview a group you will do so because of this difference – because of group psychology. Maybe you want to find out how a group (as distinct from individuals) would react to an imaginary event.

Often, the term 'focus group' is used interchangeably with 'group interview', but the two kinds of group are different:

1 In a simple **group interview**, the researcher takes a lead role, and conducts the interview with the group much as a one-to-one interview would be conducted.

2 But in a **focus group**, the researcher is more of a *facilitator*. If you run a focus group, you want to facilitate discussion among the participants, not between yourself and the participants. You assume a marginal rather than a central role.

The focus group contains eight or so participants, all with something in common (such as 'swing' voters – what they have in common is that they are all 'swingers'). It's like an unstructured interview, but with a group. Your aim is to let the *group* set the direction. Your role – as *facilitator* or *mediator* – is to stimulate discussion and make sure it stays on track.

You may do this with your comments, or with **focus materials** – such as objects, photos, drawings, newspaper stories, audio or video recordings – which the group will discuss. You may choose just to take notes, or to record in audio or on video.

20 Diaries

A diary can be more or less structured, and it can be kept by you or by your research participants. It's not an appointments diary with a little space for an entry every day. Rather, it is a record of relevant things that happen to you in the course of your research.

These are some of the things to keep in your own research diary:

- thoughts and reflections
- feelings
- actions
- new facts you have learned
- bits of conversations
- views
- interpretations.

Write up your diary straight after a session in the field. The diary can be in written note form or in audio or video recording.

If you are asking someone else to keep a diary, you can make it in whatever form records the kind of information you want from them. For example, here is one I used with teachers in asking them to keep a record of who was working alongside them in the classroom.

Mon	NA mornings (not Fri) (TA)	Mrs B (support service)	LM all pms (TA)
Tues			
Wed	⟵ Mrs T (parent) ⟶		
Thur			
Fri	⟵ Mrs P (parent) ⟶		

It doesn't have to be like this, of course. It can be informal and unstructured, just as your own could be. So, the forms of diary are as follows.

	Informal	Formal
1 Your own diary		
2 Another person's diary		

21 Questionnaires

A questionnaire is just a set of questions.
The questions may be given:

- face to face, and read out by the
  interviewer, that is, you (so this is very
  much like a structured interview)
- by phone
- sent to respondents for them to
  complete themselves: they may be
  sent by post, email or text message,
  or may be presented via social media
  such as Twitter or Facebook, or in
  other ways online.

You may be collecting facts (such as 'How many pets do you have?') or attitudes (such as 'Do you think the *Daily Star* should be reclassified as a comic?'). The questionnaire can be used in different kinds of design frame (see pp. 41–63). It can be tightly structured (as in the examples I have just given), but can also allow the opportunity for a more open-ended response if required.

Two questionnaire rules

Bear in mind these rules when drafting your questionnaire:

▶ keep it short (try to keep to one side of A4)
▶ only ask for one piece of information per question.

Kinds of questions

You can have open or closed questions:

▶ An **open question** gives free rein to the respondent to say what they want (e.g. 'Tell me what you think about the government's stance on immigration to this country').
▶ A **closed question** has to be answered with one of the alternatives that the

questioner (you) gives. Closed questions are more common in questionnaires and there is a range of ways of providing the 'closedness' of the answer.

Yes/no questions

The clue's in the name: they have to be answered 'Yes' or 'No'.

Multiple choice questions

Here, there are two or more answers and respondents are told either to tick one box, or to tick as many boxes as they like. For example:

Which of the following news channels have you watched in the last 4 weeks? Tick as many as you like.

Al Jazeera	☐
BBC News 24	☐
Bloomberg	☐
CNN	☐
France 24	☐
Russia Today	☐
Sky News	☐
Other	☐ *Please specify* _____
None	☐

Rank order questions

Here, your respondents, that is, people whom you are questioning, have to put items in rank order – from best to worst, most important to least important, most difficult to least difficult, or most beautiful to least beautiful and so on. For example, if you were interested in the factors that were most significant for parents who had just chosen a secondary school for their child, you might ask them to rank some alternatives that you set out for them, thus:

> *Thinking about the choice you have just made about your child's secondary school, please look at this list of factors and rank the three which were most important for you in making your decision. Please mark 1, 2 and 3 in the relevant boxes: 1 for most important, 2 for next most important, 3 for next most important.*

Ease of access	☐
Reputation	☐
Exam results	☐
Quality of buildings	☐
Opinion of daughter/son	☐
Opinion after visiting	☐
School prospectus	☐
Other (please elaborate)	☐ _____ _____

Rating scale questions

The respondent will rate something – an experience, attitude, attribute and so on –
along a continuum. For example:

If you have a headache, how effective do you find these painkillers?

	Very good	Good	Not much use	Useless	Never tried it
Aspirin					
Paracetamol/ acetaminophen					
Ibuprofen					
Co-codamol					

The respondent will tick only one box in each row.

The Likert scale

A Likert scale (named after the psychologist Rensis Likert) can be used in any situation
where belief or attitude is being measured. You ask for agreement or disagreement
with a *statement* you provide, as shown below. The respondent will tick only one box
in each row.

	Strongly agree	Agree	Disagree	Strongly disagree
1 Everyone should be given another chance, no matter what their crime.				
2 Some crimes are so serious that they should always carry a prison sentence.				
3 The police should be given stronger stop and search powers.				

Questionnaires online

One of the best known online questionnaire services is SurveyMonkey, at www.surveymonkey.com. At the time of writing, it lets you construct your own questionnaire free for up to 100 respondents and gives help on the construction of a questionnaire, with 24-hour online support. If you need an alternative service that lets you survey more people, you will probably find that your university subscribes to one.

22 Observation

In order to observe we need to watch (and listen) carefully, and we can do this in some very different ways. You can either observe systematically, looking for particular kinds of behaviour, or you can observe informally, a bit like a spy. Thus, we have:

1 A systematic kind of observation called **structured observation**.
2 An informal kind of observation called **unstructured observation**.

Structured observation

With **structured observation**, you are assuming that you can split the world into bits: bits that you can count. This includes even the world of people's behaviour. So, first you have to define what these bits will be. They may be bits of action, language or behaviour. Then you have to think of some way of counting how often these bits happen. Let me give an example.

Students' drinking habits

Imagine that you are interested in student drinking habits and whether males drink more than females – and, if so, whether this is related to frequency and speed of drinking when in a bar or pub. You decide to assess actual drinking behaviour. In other words: what kinds of drinking behaviour do students actually engage in?

You decide to assess this by observing how often individuals in a group of ten students, five female and five male, are actually holding their glasses at a particular moment in time. Then, *at that moment*, you will put a tick for each one holding a glass. You'll end up with a chart a bit like this.

	1 min	2 min	3 min	4 min	5 min	6 min	7 min	8 min	9 min	10 min
Emily				✓					✓	
Naz			✓							✓
Hannah								✓		✓
Josh	✓	✓			✓				✓	
Maddy		✓								
Chris							✓		✓	
Ghazala							✓			
Nico	✓	✓			✓				✓	
Sarah				✓						
Joe				✓		✓	✓			

You will end up with, for each student, a percentage of time 'drink-holding' (calculated by number of ticks divided by total number of possible ticks for each student × 100). For example, if a student obtains 3 ticks out of a possible 10 – such as Joe in the chart – then 3/10 × 100 means the student was drink-holding for 30% of the time.

This is just one way of doing structured observation – it's called 'interval recording', since you make a record (draw a tick) depending on an interval (in this case one minute, as if a *Ping!* is going off in your ear at each minute interval).

Other kinds of structured recording can be by 'duration recording' – measuring the overall time a behaviour is occurring (so, for example, timing with a stopwatch the actual length of time Emily is holding a glass over the ten minutes, then Naz, etc.); or 'frequency count recording' – recording the actual number of times each person in the group picks up their glass. If you decide to use structured recording, try to work out which would be best for your research question.

Unstructured observation

With **unstructured observation** there's *no* breaking the world down into bits that you count. Unstructured observation goes naturally with ethnography (see p. 55), because ethnography is about *participant observation*. In other words, you become part of the situation you are observing, and the trick is to make the observations as naturally as possible. You:

- watch, discreetly
- interview people
- reflect on your own experiences
- keep a diary.

All this constitutes unstructured observation and it can happen in the natural and biological sciences as well as in the social sciences. The excellent website on research method for scientists, www.engageinresearch.ac.uk/index.html, gives the example of Dian Fossey's observational work with mountain gorillas in Rwanda. What she did was rather like the work of the ethnographer doing unstructured observation – she actually became accepted by the gorillas and was able to record their behaviour in extraordinary detail. With her work she made huge contributions to the understanding of gorilla ecology, demography and social organisation.

You can collect **secondary data** – official statistics – from a wide range of sources nowadays. And you can copy them straight into your Excel file from an online source.

Try these sources:

- For the Department for Education (DfE) statistics website, google 'DfE Research & Statistics Gateway Home'. By the time you read this, the DfE may have a new title, so be intelligent in your googling.
- If you want to do comparisons between countries, Gapminder is an excellent website, which produces animated scatterplots of features of different countries, such as income per person plotted against life expectancy. Try it at www.gapminder.org/. It can be as shocking as it is fascinating.
- To get population pyramids from different countries, use www.census.gov/ipc/. These show bar charts of different countries' populations in different age bands; they are called 'pyramids' because they are usually pyramid shaped. However, with richer countries and ageing populations, they may not be.

- The European Social Survey offers a mine of information at http://ess.nsd.uib.no/, as does the Organisation for Economic Co-operation and Development website at http://stats.oecd.org.
- Local social statistics on almost anything in the UK can be found at www.neighbourhood.statistics.gov.uk/dissemination/.
- Emma Smith's website, www.secondarydataanalysis.com, takes you to a wide range of UK, US and international websites. See also her book, *Using secondary data in educational and social research* (Smith 2008).

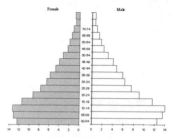

Used with permission from the US Census Bureau

| 1 Have you thought about what kind of data you can collect? | What kinds of data are these? Write down the kinds here. |
| 2 Have you decided the method you will use to collect data? | What is this? Write it down here. |

5 ANALYSING THE DATA

Once you've got all your data, what do you do with them? Remember that they are only data until you have analysed them and used them intelligently. Only then will your *data* become *evidence*. So, how do you do the analysis? Your data are likely to come in one of two main forms:

▶ words
▶ numbers.

You treat different kinds of data in different ways. Let's look at each in turn.

25 Words

What is sometimes called 'qualitative research' is usually research to do with words (or, sometimes, images). When I say 'words', I mean words joined up in the way that we usually join them up in language in our everyday lives. I don't mean isolated words, counted, as you might count them, with questionnaire responses. I mean proper sentences with meanings. How do you analyse these, other than by just taking the sentences at face value and copying them out into your research report?

Most ways of analysing words are based on the **constant comparative method**. It's all you need to know. Here's what it is.

The basic recipe for constant comparative method – step by step

1 You will need: your notes, diaries, any recordings; some different coloured highlighters; a pad of A4 paper; a pen; a computer.
2 You first read all your data: interview notes, diaries, notes from observations and so on.

3 With the highlighters, highlight parts you think are important. Use different colours for different kinds of 'important'. You'll begin to get an impression of key ideas or subjects that are coming up again and again. You can call these your **temporary constructs**. Make a list of them.

4 Now read through the data again, using your list of temporary constructs against which to compare (this is the *constant comparative* bit). Now make up a grid with the temporary constructs in the left-hand column and page numbers of where the temporary construct is mentioned in your data in the right-hand column. You can make notes and observations on the grid as you do this.

5 Delete any temporary constructs that are not earning their keep. In other words, if the temporary construct is not appearing again and again, remove it from your list.

6 Now, after your second reading, make a list of **second-order constructs** that seem to explain your data. With them you should be able to summarise the important themes in your data.

7 If you are satisfied after a final look through your data, you can label these as your **themes**.

8 Think about the themes. How do they seem to be connecting together? What matches with what? Are there any unanimous areas of agreement? Are there any contradictions or paradoxes?

9 Garnish: find ways of **visually representing** your themes – think, for example, about how you could draw them in the shape of a storyboard, or something like it, as shown on p. 25.

10 Place as part of your analysis chapter.

These **themes** or **categories** are the walls and shapes that you build out of your data. Your data are the bricks and the themes are what you make of them. Your job when you are using words in this way is to find the meanings that people are putting into the words. It is these meanings that you have to think about.

There are various ways in which you can draw diagrams of your themes to show how one is connected to another. I have outlined elsewhere (Thomas 2017) how this can be done with **network analysis** and **construct mapping**.

Using your brain (in analysing documents, for example)

Sometimes – for example, if you are doing research in history – there is no special route to analysing the data you are finding, usually from documents and books. Here, I'm afraid, the advice is simply to use your brain. The key is to find the right documents, read them carefully, and then think about them.

It's not just in historical research that documents are important. They are important across the humanities and the arts subjects and also in social science (and even natural science, sometimes). All documents are different, so it is tricky to give general advice. However, there are one or two ways in which, in a digital age, documents can be examined more easily than once was the case.

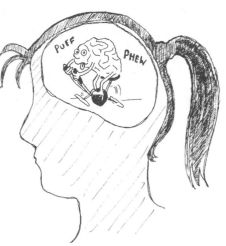

You can download documents quite easily now, particularly those from the government and other big organisations. This is especially easy if the document is in Word; and even if it is in a PDF you can, after checking copyright, copy it and then paste it into Word for fine-grain interrogation.

Tips for interrogating documents
▶ To copy everything in a PDF file, press Ctrl A while in the PDF, which 'selects all'; then press Ctrl C, which copies it (to your clipboard). Then open a blank Word document and paste the whole lot into the new Word document with Ctrl V.
▶ Learn to use a scanner. If you only have a hard copy of a document, try scanning relevant parts. Most of today's scanners have optical character recognition software. Ask the scanner to 'read' the page you need (rather than simply taking a picture of it). You can save this text into a Word file. (Make sure you check copyright restrictions first.)
▶ Use your computer to help you analyse your text, by using, for example, the Find facility (Ctrl F).

Eyeballing

Eyeballing just means looking at your numbers to see what they tell you. What do they seem to say? Are they going up or down? Are they all around one point? Are there any that seem not to fit with the others?

Your eyeball (teaming up with your brain) is your most valuable tool in dealing with numbers and you should trust it. Sometimes, it seems to me that we trust statistics too much – we should rely on our common sense as well as the statistics to tell us what a range of numbers may be saying.

Explaining

The second thing to remember with numbers is that the numbers and the statistics used to analyse them serve no function in themselves. They have no intrinsic merit. They help you to analyse, but this analysis exists in order for you to explain, discuss and communicate your findings. So, remember that when you present an analysis using numbers, you will need to explain with words. Tell your readers what you want them to see in the numbers: the **statistics don't speak for themselves**.

	Mites	Ants	Arths
Set 1	132	456	206
Set 2	121	410	314

This table tells us that [blah blah blah] and indicates that [blah blah blah]. We may infer from it [blah blah blah].

The table below provides a brief résumé of descriptive statistics you might use.

Presentation	Good for …	Comment	
1 Column graph	▶ comparing values ▶ ranking top to bottom	This example shows number of hospital admissions for hip fractures among women in various age bands.	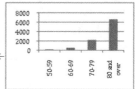
2 Bar chart	▶ comparing values ▶ ranking top to bottom	Since it is presented 'on its side', readers don't have to turn their heads to read long labels.	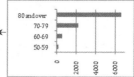
3 Line chart	comparing values over time	Be careful about these. Sometimes it is not correct to draw a line, i.e. there is *not* always a *link* between one value and the next. This example shows the rise in the numbers of teaching assistants (in thousands) from 1997 to 2007.	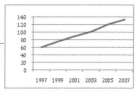

Presentation	Good for ...	Comment	
4 Pie chart	comparing each value with the total value	Think about what you are using it for. For example, it's *not* worth showing just two values (like 59% female, 41% male) in a pie chart, as it's just as easy to read the numbers.	←
5 Scatter chart	comparing pairs of values	For a class of schoolchildren, you may be collecting data on two variables, such as age and reading age (in months).	←

The five methods of descriptive statistics described in the table above comprise the more commonly used ways of presenting numbers visually. They are used surprisingly little by students doing research. Do remember your readers and remember that you:

▶ need to make things intelligible for them, and
▶ must demonstrate that you can think intelligently about numbers and how they can best be presented.

So, consider how best to present your numbers meaningfully. If you are using numbers in your work and you don't know how to use Microsoft Excel, you really need to find out how, as Excel provides a range of charts you can use. There are some very clear tutorials on YouTube; look especially for tutorials that explain how to use the 'Charts' function.

Here, I have described descriptive statistics (because they describe), but there are of course others that have different purposes. The kind of statistic that you might use when doing an experiment is outlined on p. 60. If you are using these statistics, you will probably need to use SPSS rather than Excel. SPSS is available on most university pooled computers.

1 Have you thought about what kind of analysis you need in the light of the data you have collected?	What kind of analysis is this? Write the answer down here.
2 Have you decided the method you will use to analyse data?	What is this? Write it down here.

WRITING UP RESEARCH

Your reader (that is, your marker) will have clear expectations about what a research write-up should look like – what you should write and the order in which it should appear.

All research is different so all write-ups are different. But here is a rough summary of what might be in a typical write up.

Chapter 1 Introduction

The introduction explains your interest in the topic of the study. At the end of it, you can state your prima facie question(s) (see p. 9).

Chapter 2 Literature

The literature review says what other research has been done in the area. This lets you refine your prima facie research question(s).

Chapter 3 Method

A methodology chapter explains why you have chosen to do your research in this way. Say why you have done, for example, an action research project and a questionnaire. It's important to say *why* you have chosen these rather than simply describing them.

Chapter 4 Findings

Say what you actually found here.

Chapter 5 Analysis and discussion

Here, you analyse your findings using the tools outlined in Part 5. You will go on to discuss your analysis in the context of your research questions and in the light of any issues raised in the literature review.

Chapter 6 Conclusion

In the conclusion you will draw together the threads and offer the reader an assessment of how well your questions have been answered. (See also *Report writing* in this series.)

Here are the rough proportions and corresponding numbers of words given to each of these sections, although I should warn you that this is only a rough guide: some write-ups will be very different. Don't feel straitjacketed by this.

Chapters	Proportion of the whole write-up (%)	Words in a 10,000-word project write-up
1 Introduction	5	500
2 Literature review	25	2,500
3 Methodology	15	1,500
4 Fieldwork and findings	20	2,000
5 Analysis and discussion	30	3,000
6 Conclusion	5	500

Just a few pages, no more

Lots of writing but, remember, not a list

Longer than you think it needs to be; explain why you did it this way

The guts

More guts

Just a few pages, no more

Chapters 4 and 5 in this imaginary write-up can present a bit of a problem in knowing how best to present them. With a scientific study in chemistry or biology or certain kinds of psychology experiment, you will present your chapters as neatly divided, like this. You may even separate fieldwork and findings into two separate chapters.

However, in many kinds of research in the social sciences, particularly those involving case study, it is difficult to decide how Chapters 4 and 5 should be presented. Should they be two chapters, as above, or – given the wholeness stressed by a case study – should you present these as one chapter? All the time as you are presenting your findings, you will be testing them out against your thoughts and reflections – in other words, against your analysis. So, all this should be in one chapter rather than two. The difference between these kinds of study is shown below. (See also *Planning your dissertation* in this series.)

A research write-up in biology or chemistry, or some psychology projects	Findings →	analysis →	discussion
A write-up of an ethnography or a piece of case study research in any field	Findings, analysis and discussion		

One of the questions the examiners will keep asking themselves of your research is: 'Does this research address the title?' Perhaps the commonest cause of low marks is when a piece of work – research project or essay – doesn't address the title.

So, it is best to proceed with a working title – a provisional one – until you get to the end, and then revise this to your final title. *You* can then make sure that the work addresses the title, because it is *you* who have decided what the title is going to be. This is one of the nice things about doing research (as distinct from doing an essay) at university – you're the boss: you can decide what it is about.

It is easier to address your title if it is in two parts, with the first part giving the general context and the second part specifying more exactly the focus of your interest. For example:

> Paternalism and adversarialism in the British press: the influence of Beaverbrook and Rothermere on today's media

or

> Cognitive dissonance in the preschool child: case studies of six children

29 Writing an abstract

An abstract comprises one (or maybe two or three) paragraph, usually totalling 150–300 words, which gives a summary of your research. It should be your research in a nutshell. In being your research in a nutshell, it should say everything that your research has been about, *including your findings*. The last bit is important, because many students leave out their findings, as if these weren't important. I have no idea why.

You should take the writing of your abstract very seriously because it is your readers' first impression of your work – and first impressions count. And if your readers need reminding (as they might) of what your research is about as they read, they may well turn back to the abstract.

So, the abstract is a summary of the project, containing a review of your:

▶ questions
▶ methods
▶ findings
▶ conclusions.

Write the abstract when you have finished the whole project, for the same reason that you write your title when you have finished. It's only at the end that you can decide what should be in there. Although you write it at the end, you put the abstract at the beginning, right after the title page. It is so important that it has a page all to itself.

See also *Planning your dissertation* (Chapter 23) in this series.

There are some important rules for writing up research:

▶ Remember your reader – remember that someone is reading your work.
▶ Read it out loud. Does it sound right? Can *you* understand what you mean?
▶ Draft and edit. Then do it again. Then do it again (and so on).
▶ Proofread your work. Ask someone else to proofread it too.
▶ Number your pages. In Word, go to Insert, then Page Numbers.
▶ Use 35 mm (1.5 inches) margins on the left, and 25 mm (1 inch) on the right, top and bottom. Or follow your own university guidelines.
▶ Double-space your work, as specified by most university regulations. Select all (Ctrl A), then press Ctrl 2.
▶ If you quote someone else's work, you must always attribute their work, otherwise it is plagiarism. If you use a quotation of 40 words or longer, indent it, without quotation marks. If shorter, keep it in the text and put quotation marks around it.
▶ Make sure you 'reference' work you refer to in your write-up. All university libraries tell you how to use the Harvard method for referencing.

See also *Referencing and understanding plagiarism* in this series.

	✓ or ✗
1 Have you organised your work into chapters?	
2 Have you sketched out how your work will divide between the chapters?	
3 Have you decided, finally, on a title?	
4 Have you written an abstract?	
5 Have you got hold of your university's regulations on referencing and presentation and made sure you conform to them?	

References and useful sources

References

Booth WC, Colomb GC, Williams JM (2008). *The craft of research* (3rd edn). Chicago: University of Chicago Press.

Cooper H, Shoolbred M (2016). *Where's your argument?* London: Palgrave.

Field A (2013). *Discovering statistics using IBM SPSS statistics* (4th edn). London: SAGE.

Geertz C (1975). *The interpretation of cultures*. London: Hutchinson.

Godwin J (2014). *Planning your essay* (2nd edn). Basingstoke: Palgrave Macmillan.

Hammersley M, Gomm R (2000). Introduction. In M Gomm, M Hammersley and P Foster (eds), *Case study method*. London: SAGE.

McNiff J (2016). *You and your action research project* (4th edn). London: Routledge.

Reid M (2012) *Report writing*. Basingstoke: Palgrave Macmillan.

Sacks O (1996). *An anthropologist on Mars*. London: Picador.

Smith E (2008). *Using secondary data in educational and social research*. Maidenhead: Open University Press.

Thomas G (2016). *How to do your case study* (2nd edn). London: SAGE.

Thomas G (2017). *How to do your research project: a guide for students in education and applied social sciences* (3rd edn). London: SAGE.

Van der Ham V (2016). *Analyzing a case study*. London: Palgrave.

Williams K (2013). *Planning your dissertation*. Basingstoke: Palgrave Macmillan.

Williams K (2014). *Getting critical (*2nd edn). Basingstoke: Palgrave Macmillan.

Williams K, Davis M (2017). *Referencing and understanding plagiarism* (2nd edn). London: Palgrave.

Useful sources

Becker HS (2007). *Writing for social scientists: how to start and finish your thesis, book, or article* (2nd edn). Chicago: Chicago University Press.

Good on writing and writing-up.

Engage in Research: www.engageinresearch.ac.uk/index.html.

This website is primarily directed at bioscience students and gives excellent step-by-step advice.

McNiff J (2016). *You and your action research project* (4th edn). London: Routledge.

Good, practical advice on action research from a renowned expert.

Oliver P (2010). *The student's guide to research ethics* (2nd edn). Maidenhead: Open University Press.

Excellent book that covers just about everything you need to know on ethics.

Pears R, Shields G (2016). *Cite them right* (10th edn). London: Palgrave.

Especially good on the problems of referencing internet sources.

Research Methods Knowledge Base: www.socialresearchmethods.net/kb/.

Good online overview of experimental design and probability.

Ridley D (2012). *The literature review: a step-by-step guide for students* (2nd edn). London: SAGE.

Very helpful advice on creating a narrative from your review.

Salkind NJ (2016). *Statistics for people who (think they) hate statistics*. Thousand Oaks, CA: SAGE.

My favourite book on statistics, with lots of cartoons.

Smith E (2008). *Using secondary data in educational and social research*. Maidenhead: Open University Press.

Invaluable sourcebook for official statistics and how you can use them.

Thomas G (2016). *How to do your case study: a guide for students and researchers* (2nd edn). London: SAGE.

Here, I have tried to guide the case inquirer through the process of doing a case study.

White P (2008). *Developing research questions: a guide for social scientists*. Basingstoke: Palgrave Macmillan.

Lots of good advice on the research question in social science.

Index